I0416759

How to Start a Pop-Up Shop

Learn an Exciting Way to Expand Your Business

Brielle Cadogan

Please consult a licensed professional before attempting any techniques outlined in this book.

By reading this document, the reader agrees that under no circumstances is the author responsible for any losses, direct or indirect, that are incurred as a result of the use of information contained within this document, including, but not limited to, errors, omissions, or inaccuracies.

Table of Contents

Introduction

My guess is that you're running your own e-commerce business right now. You have an online presence, but for one reason or another, you're interested in the idea of starting a pop-up shop. Maybe you want to try and drum up some extra sales, you have some backstock you want to try and get rid of, or you want to test the waters for a brick-and-mortar store. Whatever your reasons are for wanting to start a pop-up shop, you're in the right place. Even if you haven't started your business yet and you're looking at opening by starting off with a pop-up shop, you're still in the right place. In this book, my goal is to cover everything you need to know about a pop-up shop. You're going to learn how to spot a good pop-up shop event because they're not all created equal. You're also going to learn how to make the most of your time leading up to the event to ensure every little detail is in place. Of course, you're going to learn some strategies you can utilize to maximize profit during the event, and a whole lot more in between. I'm sure you're eager to learn more so let's go ahead and get things popping!

Chapter 1: Are Pop-Up Shops Even Worth It?

Before we get into anything else, it's first important to discuss why I believe that pop-up shops are a great idea for any type of product that you're selling. Well, I should say that it could be a great chance for you to sell more products. You see, as with anything in business, operating your business isn't free. You're going to spend money to be at the event. You're going to spend money setting up your area, and that's not even to mention all of the time that's going to go into planning and setting everything up. So this is not some small thing that you just want to have a carefree attitude with. Taking that approach to things will certainly have you leaving frustrated and with barely any profit. It is a good idea to stop and think about if this is going to be the right move for your business. It probably is, but either way, these are some of the reasons why pop-up shops are something that can help to benefit your business if you predominately have an online presence at the moment.

Gives You a Chance to Expand Your Customer Base

Yes, the current world we live in is a digital world and that's not going to change. People do love to shop online, but people also like to get out of the house and do their shopping in person. If you choose a good location, there are going to be people at the event. They're going to walk by your shop and see you in person. You're gaining exposure to people who otherwise would never know that you existed. You're essentially working double time. Your website is up 24/7 to help create exposure for your business. Your social media posts work hard to create brand awareness. At the same time, while those things are happening online, you can be in a physical location to help create even more exposure for your brand. Now if you do things correctly, your shop can have a lasting effect on the people who do stop by. There's something special about seeing something in person compared to online. Therefore, the likelihood of creating a loyal customer who will buy from you again and again will be increased because people will be able to experience your products firsthand, instead of just seeing a picture or video online.

People Get to Experience Your Products in Person

Like I briefly talked about in my previous point, people getting to experience your products in person is a big deal. Let's say, for example, you're selling something like candles, soap, or some other type of product that's based on scent. Sure, online you can describe what the scent is and people will have a general idea as to what the product could smell like. We all have an idea of what lavender smells like, but lavender products don't all smell exactly the same. So when people are shopping online, they're not able to have that experience in person and instead, they have to imagine it, and that's not as powerful. Someone can walk into your pop-up shop, pick up one of your candles, and smell it for themselves. They'll either be hooked or know that scent isn't for them. When people have a chance to experience something in person, it's going to have a bigger impact on them.

Trust is Higher

People are more trusting when shopping in person compared to shopping online. Sure, there are trusted brands out there, where someone knows they can put in their credit card information and get the item that they paid for. Most websites don't have that type of trust because people don't know who they are. They'll come across the website and they have to trust that they'll get what they paid for. They also have to trust that they'll be able to return the items if it doesn't work out. First-time visitors to a website aren't going to waste a bunch of time to try and figure out what the return policy is, for example. They're going to make snap judgments based on things like your website design, and that will determine if they buy or not. When it comes to shopping in person, yes people will still make snap judgments, but you have more leeway with things. People will be able to see and experience your product in person, which can help to do a lot of the selling for you. When people shop retail in person, they also know that they're going to get the product they're paying for because no shipping is involved. So if you've been struggling to generate some sales online recently, doing a pop-up shop can help to drive some sales because of the higher trust, and these customers will be more likely to buy from your online store because they know that they can trust you.

Good Way to Test the Waters

Having a pop-up is an inexpensive way to test things out if you are thinking about starting a store with a physical location one day. There are a lot of things that go into a physical store that are different from operating online. So if a brick-and-mortar store is something that you're currently on the fence about, there really isn't a better way to ensure if this is the right move for you. Sure, your pop-up shop will be on a smaller scale when compared to an actual brick-and-mortar, but you'll still gain the experience of having to set up your shop and having to think about how you present your products, and how you want the layout of your store to be.

Can Move Old Inventory That You Need to Get Rid Of

In business sometimes certain products don't sell as well as we'd like for them to. Having a pop-up shop is a great way to get rid of some of the extra inventory that you have that's starting to take up too much space. The reason why you can efficiently move old products is because you can put deals on it. For instance, if you're selling clothing, you could mark the items you're trying to get rid of quickly as buy 1 get 1 free, or really anything that you want. You could do buy 1 get 2 free or 5 free. It's your business, so you can do what you want, and you can make an insane deal if you're really trying to get rid of some of your backstock. You could even ramp up your deal as the day goes on. So at the start of the day, your deal could be buy 1 get 1 free. By the end of the day, things could have increased to buy 1 get 3 free, for example. Yes, you can set deals up like this online, but doing this in person creates more of a sense of urgency. People are out and about looking around, so they're already in the mood to buy. Secondly, they know that your pop-up store isn't going to stay there, so it really creates this now or never type of mentality.

Good Way to Make Extra Cash Quickly

Pop-up shops are an effective way to put cash in your pocket. If the pop-up event is a single day, you could easily make hundreds or even thousands in profit depending on the venue. How much money you're able to make will come down to a variety of different factors, with the main one being the location itself. However, even if you have a stellar location, your shop could still flop if things aren't aesthetically pleasing, or if there are other frustrations your customers will face, such as you not accepting a certain form of payment. Just imagine though if you cracked the one thousand dollar mark from a one-day pop-up shop. If most people could make that from a day of work they'd be pretty happy, and if the conditions are right, you can do just that. All things considered, the cost is low and the potential to make good money is high, so a pop-up shop is a no-brainer. There will be some things that you'll need to purchase such as racks or tables, but once you have those items, you'll be able to use them time and time again for any future pop-up shops that you might do.

Chapter 2: How to Find a Good Pop-Up Shop for Your Business

In this chapter, I want to cover some different ways you can go about finding different venues for your pop-up shop. In the next chapter, I'm going to cover some strategies you can use to determine if a certain spot is going to be a good fit for you or not. You can't do research on a venue if you don't know of any events that are going on in the first place, so this is where we have to start.

What Type of Pop-Up Shop Do You Want to Run?

The first thing you need to think about is the type of pop-up shop that you want to run. There's a wide range when it comes to pop-up shops. You could have a pop-up shop for a day, a weekend, or for a longer time period, such as a few weeks or a few months. Typically, if your pop-up shop is going to be for a shorter period of time, your area will usually be smaller. This is because your shop will likely be part of a larger event where each person will have their own designated space. If you're going to have a pop-up shop that lasts for a longer period of time, this will usually involve leasing space for a short period of time and you'll have more space to work with. These are generalizations because you could sublease a small space from a current business for 3 months, for example. If you're looking at potentially starting your own brick-and-mortar store, having a pop-up shop in a bigger space for a longer period of time makes more sense. This will allow you to better replicate what it would be like to have an actual storefront. If you're trying to quickly get rid of some extra inventory or make some quick cash, a shorter time frame pop-up shop will make more sense for you. You'll want to determine this before anything else, as this will change how you go about finding places for your pop-up shop.

Look for Now Leasing Signs

The first method that I want to talk about is going to be if you want to have a pop-up shop that lasts for a longer period of time. You'll first want to determine roughly how many square feet you want your shop to be. You don't want to lease a space that's too big for what you need, and being too small isn't going to serve you well either. What you'll want to do is drive around and look for "now leasing" signs on commercial retail properties. Even if you don't see a sign, you can still look for places that are moving or going out of business. What you'll want to do is contact the property manager and see if there are any openings or spots opening up soon. The other place you'll want to look at are malls. Malls are a great hub where businesses move in and out regularly, so it's easy to get in contact with the manager and determine what's open and what will be open soon. Lastly, even if you're coming across places that don't appear to have any openings, it wouldn't hurt anything to contact the property manager to see if something might be opening up soon. Even if you don't feel that you're ready to move in yet, you'll want to go ahead and start the process of finding a place. It can take a while for everything to fall into place, so you'll want to start looking well in advance of when you feel that you're ready. This is more so true if you're looking to have a space for a longer period of time than a one-day pop-up that's a part of an event. It's more tricky because it can be harder to find month-to-month or 3-month lease options, as opposed to multiple years. A property manager would rather have the stability of knowing a business is going to be there for a while, as opposed to only a few short months, and then have to try and find someone else to fill the void.

Hire a Professional

The go-to way to find a short lease option for your pop-up shop would be to work with a professional like a commercial real estate agent. This isn't necessary if your pop-up shop is part of a small event, as you can find these places on your own and there's nothing to negotiate. For finding the right-sized space, for the right price, and the correct term length, hiring a real estate agent makes a lot of sense. You can go ahead and breathe easy because, as the buyer, you're not going to be paying any commissions, the seller is. The thing about working with a real estate agent is that this is their field. They've built the connections and have a good understanding of the local area. They'll know what's available, what isn't, and what will become available soon enough. So doing this can take a big weight off of your shoulders. Even after you give them the criteria you're looking for, such as 2,000 square feet of space for a 3-month term, you still need to be patient, as it can take some time to find places that fit the criteria.

Conduct Online Searches

Thankfully we are able to take advantage of advances in modern technology that allow us to make certain things easier, such as finding a spot for a pop-up shop. Regardless of what type of pop-up shop you want, conducting online searches is a good way to go about things. If you're looking for a longer-term pop-up shop, you could search for something along the lines of "available retail space for lease in 'blank' city." Maybe when you were out and about looking for available space, you came across a location that looked good, but you couldn't find information to contact the people who manage the property. You could search for the name of the strip mall or the address of the strip mall, followed by "property manager." If you're looking for something that's a smaller timeframe that's part of a bigger event, then you can search for something along the lines of "event vendors in 'blank' city," "pop-up shops in 'blank' city," "pop-up shop locations in 'blank' city," "pop-up shop availabilities near me," "flea market near me," or "event listings near me." This will give you a nice range of options that you can start looking into to see if anything will be a good fit for you.

Use Social Media

You can use social media to help act as a search engine for the purposes of finding a pop-up shop venue. You can search for the same phrases that you normally would on a regular search engine, and see what comes up. Depending on what platform you're using, some locations will come up as well as other creator accounts. It's a good idea to follow these accounts to see if they try out any new locations. If someone makes a video about trying out a pop-up shop, leave a comment and ask them what their location was because you're interested in starting your own pop-up shop as well. Also, follow your city's social media page or any other vendor pages, and keep a close eye on things for any future events that they may post about. Most cities will also have an event calendar that they keep updated on their website, so it's a good idea to take a look at that, not just for the city you live in but the surrounding areas as well. There's no point in limiting your options if you are willing to travel a little bit.

Drive Around

Just like how you can drive around looking for spots that are available to lease, you can do the same thing when looking for a shorter-term pop-up spot. The best way to go about doing this is to look around on a Saturday, as that's when most of these events will be taking place. Start by driving around any downtown areas and then moving outwards from there, and see if you come across anything. Once you do find something, see if you can find the name of the event or who's running it. If you're not able to, then ask some of the sellers who you need to get in contact with so that you can participate in a future event that this vendor might hold in the future.

Ask People in Your Network

People in your current network may know of upcoming events or they may have participated in events themselves as a seller in the past. If there's someone you know of off the top of your head, you can reach out to that person directly. If not, the best way to approach this is to post on your personal social media profiles. A simple post such as the following can go a long way:

"Hey everyone, as you may or may not know I've been running my own ecommerce store where I sell body care products. I'm looking to participate in a single-day pop-up shop to give my customers a chance to experience some of my products in person. If you know of any upcoming vendor events in the city that are looking for small businesses to participate, please send me a direct message. I would greatly appreciate it!"

At first glance, doing something like this might seem like a waste of time, but you don't know what your network knows. A lot of the people that you're friends with you likely don't know everything there is to know about them. You also probably don't know what they've been up to recently. Someone could have gotten a new job working for the city or a venue that's putting on an event, and now they could be the perfect connection for you. You simply won't know unless you give it a shot. You don't have anything to lose. People will either think nothing of it and move on, or you could get some good information from it. There's nothing to be embarrassed about, so lean on your network and let them assist you!

Use Online Forums and Groups

Posting in online forums and groups is another good way to use the network of a local community to see what is going on in the city. You can join Facebook groups that are related to your city and make a post similar to the example I just gave for posting on your personal profiles. The same thing goes for online forums. It can be a good way to get insider knowledge that you likely wouldn't have known about. You have no idea who's in these groups, so there's a chance that someone is in there who has the information that you're looking for.

Approach Other Businesses

The cool thing about a pop-up shop is that it doesn't just have to be something where there are a bunch of other sellers around you and everyone is there as part of some bigger thing. Instead, a pop-up shop could be as simple as a fold-out table outside of someone's business. Seriously, it can get that simple. You can take advantage of someone else's business, and this works as a plus for both you and the business. The business might have some extra space on the inside or the outside of their operation, and it will allow them to make some extra money. For you, this will give you the opportunity to gain new exposure for your business and make some extra cash. You're essentially going to be piggybacking off of the foot traffic that walks by or goes inside of that business or the surrounding area. This is more common than you think. Just the other week I went out to eat and there was an organization with a table outside asking for donations to help end child abuse. So you can most definitely do the same thing to sell more of your product. The only way that this will happen though is if you go out and talk to businesses to see if they might be interested. The thought of this might scare you, but the good news is that you don't necessarily have to approach in person if you don't feel comfortable with that. You can call or email as well. You'll want to start off by mentioning who you are and that you're interested in creating a small one-day pop-up shop in front of the business, or possibly on the inside, if space allows. It's also important to mention that you're of course willing to pay for being there and mention approximately how much space you plan on taking up. If you say you only plan on having a fold-out table, this will give the business a good idea of how much space it's going to take to accommodate you.

You don't want to mention how much you'd be willing to pay, instead leave it open-ended, and end your pitch by asking if this is something they might be interested in. See if they bring up a price in their response back to you. If they do throw out a number for how much they would want, this can give you a good idea to know if you're in the same ballpark with the number that you had in mind. If they don't toss out a number, that's okay, they might ask how much you'd be willing to pay when they respond back to you. Go ahead and give them a number. How much you should offer will depend on how busy the area is and where you're located. Typically a good range is $100-$300 for the day, but it all will depend on the location. If you live in New York City, for example, you're going to be paying far more than that, so just expect that ahead of time. This is why I recommend that you start by hitting up places you're already familiar with. Start with places that you know get a lot of foot traffic. If you reach out to places that are in areas you're unaware of, that's not a deal breaker. You can go to these areas on the day of the week when you'll have your pop-up shop, and scope out the foot traffic for yourself. This will give you a good idea of how much you should offer, as the last thing you want to do is overpay for a spot that doesn't generate much foot traffic. A good place to start with this is your network, once again. Do you know of anyone who operates their own business with a physical location? It could be anything. Maybe someone you know operates a restaurant, flower shop, or car wash. Any place that has foot traffic can be good and your friend will likely not charge a lot for the opportunity. They'll also be more likely to say yes, which is a big plus as well.

Trade Shows

Depending on what it is that you're selling, a trade show can be a great way to get in front of your targeted customer base. Depending on what the event is, you don't know what type of people will be showing up. However, if there's a body care convention, then you know that the type of people who are going to be showing up are the ones who care about body care products. So if you're selling body care products, then do a search for body care trade shows near me, upcoming body care conventions, or other variations along those lines. You'll pay a fee to have your own space, and boom now you get to take advantage of the highly targeted foot traffic.

Ask Other Sellers at Events

Once you're at your first pop-up shop location regardless of if it's a trade show, flea market, event the city is putting on, or whatever else, ask other people who are selling at that event where else they've gone to sell their products. You're not going to be the only person who is trying to make some extra cash from a pop-up shop, so you might as well learn from other people who are trying to do it as well. Chances are good that they'll know of some places that you haven't thought of yet. This is a good way to build your connections and gain insight about other events that you wouldn't have found on your own. You do have to be mindful though because other people are likely going to be selling different products from you. So a location that worked out well for them might not translate well for you. Don't automatically assume a suggestion is going to be a big hit for you without doing your proper due diligence first, which is what you're about to learn how to do in the next chapter.

Chapter 3: How to Conduct Research to Ensure the Event is Right for Your Business

Finding potential locations for you to have a pop-up shop is a great start. Finding places doesn't mean much though because not all locations are created equally. Some will be more profitable for you than others, and other locations will be better for other types of businesses. The only way you'll be able to know is if you do some digging prior to. It's also important to note that conducting research gives you the best chance to know if something will be worth your time or not. Regardless, there isn't a full-proof way to know that one location is going to be way more profitable than another. Sometimes you are going to have to take a small leap of faith and learn from the experience. There's nothing wrong with this as this is how we learn as humans. Once you gain more and more experience, you'll start to get a good feel for what will be profitable and what won't be. The goal with doing research is to make the risk as small as possible, but make no mistake, there isn't a way to get rid of it completely.

How Much Will It Cost You to Be at One of the Events?

Much like in the previous chapter when I mentioned approaching other businesses, the range will vary for how much it will cost you. To rent a booth for the day, it might only cost you $50-$250 for the day. The more sellers that are going to be at the event can help to drive down prices, as there are more spots to fill. Again though, the prices you'll pay will vary quite considerably all depending on where you live. You might live in a spot where you'll have to pay a good chunk more than what I've mentioned here. If you are in an area where it's going to put a strain on your budget, then it's important to be more diligent with your research process. If it's cheaper, then you can definitely gain some hands-on experience and learn from the process to make things better for the next time. Generally speaking, the cost shouldn't be that much, which is why you can really make some good money if you approach things correctly. You are likely going to be competing with a large amount of other sellers and some of them will be selling the same type of products that you're selling. This is why it's so crucial for you to be able to stand out from the crowd, or else you won't be successful no matter what location you set up at.

Is There an Entry Fee for People to Get In?

The first thing that you're going to want to look into is an entry fee for customers. Think about your favorite retail store. When you want to shop there, do you have to pay to get into the store? No, of course you don't. Imagine if you did though. What kind of a deterrent would that be for you to shop at that store? You'd have to plan ahead and be strategic with what you wanted before you came in. If you're walking out empty-handed, then you're going to feel like you wasted your money because you paid to get in but then left with nothing. So when events make people pay to get in, it can hurt the foot traffic because people don't like to pay for things that they feel should be free. You're also not going to be making any money off of the entrance fee, so a fee hurts you more than it helps as an independent seller. However, it would be a mistake to automatically write a place off because they're charging an entry fee. Sure, an event could charge a fee because they want to make as much money as possible. After all, they don't directly care if you make money or not. They don't make more because you're making more. They make more money by having more sellers at the event and the number of people that show up to it if they're charging an entrance fee. On the flip side though, a fee could be charged because the event is just that popular. There could still be a lot of people who show up even if they have to pay to get in. Just know ahead of time that the crowd will be limited if they have to pay an entrance fee.

How Much Traffic Does the Place Get?

The next factor you'll want to consider is how much foot traffic the place is able to generate. If the place hosts sellers once per month for example, see if you can go to the event as a consumer before you sign up to be a seller. Once you get there, pay attention to the amount of people that you see. If you want to get even more strategic, you could stay in one area and count the number of people that walk by over the course of 30 minutes so that you can get an idea of how many people are visiting. I also recommend visiting during peak hours so that way you can see the place at its best. If you don't like what you see during a peak time, then you're not going to want to set up shop there. Stopping by and doing this at one place isn't going to give you much perspective. You need to do this at multiple places so you can get an idea for what's going to be a good value for your money and what isn't. For instance, one place might charge twice as much as another place but have less foot traffic. You'd never know the difference unless you actually go in person and see for yourself. Now, if a place isn't too expensive, you could just pay and go through the experience firsthand, and you'll get a feel for the amount of foot traffic that the venue is able to generate.

How Many Other Vendors Will Be There?

You also want to know what you're going to be competing against. The more people that are there selling, the more competition you're going to have for people's attention. If people have a certain budget they're trying to stick with, you're going to have to work that much harder to earn those dollars. You can figure out the number of vendors at the event by asking the host, and they should be able to tell the number of people who have signed up so far and the maximum number of slots that are available. The other way you can determine how many sellers will be at the event is by going to the event and scoping things out. This will be able to give you a good feel for how many other vendors you're going to be up against.

What Type of Sellers Are at the Event?

The number of people that come to the event is one thing, but what also matters is what the people are selling. If you sell clothing and so does everyone else, then you're going to have to be creative to stand out. Hopefully, the reason why everyone is selling clothes is because the event is marketed as a clothing event, so that way the people that come will be interested in clothes. If the event is more general, then you don't want to be competing with a bunch of other sellers who are trying to sell similar types of products to you. The people who come aren't necessarily going to be targeted for what you're selling. In addition to that, you could very well have a better setup and items compared to the next guy, but what if someone comes across their shop first simply because of their location? Sure that's out of your control, but if people are looking for clothes and they don't see many people selling clothes, then they'll have to keep looking. This will increase the likelihood that they'll stumble across your shop. In order to get a feel for what type of sellers will be there, you can ask the event host what types of businesses usually sign up. The other tried and true method is to check things out for yourself if the same event is going on before the date when you signed up. Doing this will be a good way to tell exactly what you'll be up against. I would recommend walking the entire premise and counting how many other people are selling the same type of product you are. In the end, if everything else checks out, don't let competition deter you from signing up. Competition isn't going to be something you can completely avoid and that's understandable. The good news is that you have knowledge on your side that you can use to help separate yourself from anyone who does try and sell the same type of product as you.

What Type of Shopper Comes to the Event?

Another thing you'll want to think about is the type of person that the event will attract. For example, let's say you're setting up shop in front of a high-end clothing store and you're selling used items. It's more likely that you won't be as successful because your products aren't in alignment with the location. People who would be shopping at a high-end outlet are going to be less interested in used items and would prefer to buy new. Conversely, if you're at a flea market and you're selling super high-end clothing items, then you better be ready to negotiate because people are going to be looking for a good deal. People at a flea market are much more open to buying used items because that's a good chunk of what they're expecting to see along with new items. In either scenario, it's not like you're guaranteed to fail. It's just that there could be better options for you where the chances of success will be more seamless because the quality of items that you're selling is in alignment with what the customer is expecting to see.

Does the Venue Have a Big Marketing Budget?

One of the last but certainly not least important things you'll want to look into is how the event is being marketed, if at all. With venues, it can be hit or miss as to how much they care. The way they make money is by getting as many sellers to sign up as possible. What happens after that they really don't care about, with one exception and that is the fact that sellers won't want to come back if the venue is a dud. Of course, there will always be newcomers who don't know any better and sign up. So the cycle can continue and the venue can continue to be subpar. Then there are venues that care and want to ensure the best outcome for the sellers because they know sellers will continue to come back, and it will help to drive up demand allowing them to increase prices. Marketing is an additional expense the venue is going to have to spare, but ideally, for your sake, this is something that you want to see. This will show you that the venue cares about bringing out as many people as possible to the event. Get in contact with the person or company who's putting on the event and ask what it is they're doing for marketing. In addition to that you can also search for them online and on social media. You'll at least want to see some sort of online presence, or else the average person is going to have a hard time finding them even if they would be interested in attending.

Where is the Venue Located?

One key aspect to the success of the event is its location. One reason why a venue might not have much of a marketing plan is because they won't need to. If the event is going to be held in a busy area that's naturally going to have a lot of people as is, then there isn't going to be as much of a need for marketing. People will already be in that area and they'll be able to stop by and check it out. The same thing goes if the venue is right off the side of a busy highway or road. People will be passing by and it will make it easier for people to come and see what's going on. The venue could instead be in a more remote location where people have to drive a bit out of the way to get to it. It might not be in a shopping mall area or other high-traffic location. In this case, the venue is going to be much more reliant on marketing ability to get people to come out. So if the venue is in a remote location and they don't have a big plan for marketing, that could sign that you need to stay away. But these two things aren't necessarily the final nail in the coffin.

How Established is the Event?

Certain sellers' markets are well-established and have been going on for decades. They are well-known events and people know when they occur. For example, a certain event might occur once on the first Saturday of every month. If this is the case, then people are going to be more likely to know about the event. Therefore, they might not have to do much for marketing as they can rely more on word of mouth from people who have already previously gone to the event and told their friends about it. The same applies to their location, people already know about it so even if it's more remotely located this won't be a dealbreaker because of the reliance on an established group of people. If the event is newer, then they won't have a foundation that they can lean on. So if the location is remote, there's no or very little marketing in play, and they're new, then it's probably a good idea to look elsewhere.

How Much Will It Cost You?

I've already talked about prices you can expect to pay for a one-day pop-up shop, but price is important to think about as part of your decision-making process. If all of the pieces of the puzzle check out, then it will naturally make sense for a venue to charge you more to have a spot. This isn't a bad thing as you can be more sure that it's going to be worth your time if you execute properly. The thing is that if you don't have any experience, it can be worth going to a cheaper place just to get your feet wet with the process. Going for a place that checks most of the boxes and is cheaper could be a better first choice than something that is pricier if budget is of concern to you. All-in-all, it's important to consider all of these factors along with the cost to you in order to help you determine what will be the best value. Think about which location will give you the highest quality customers, the biggest volume of customers, and the cheapest price. That's the ideal blend that you want to look for when doing your research. You're not always going to find the perfect place, but you're already getting a leg up on other sellers by at least doing research in the first place instead of jumping into things blindly.

Chapter 4: How to Prepare for the Day of Your Pop-Up Shop

We've finally arrived at the fun part. This is where you're going to learn how to make the most of your pop-up shop. If you've done everything right up to this point, all you have to do is take care of some small details and everything else should fall into place. The location is the most important factor though, so be sure to take that seriously. The goal of this chapter is to get you to think about some other aspects of a pop-up shop that you might not have thought about. It's better to learn about these things now rather than your first shop be a failure because you forgot to think about a few critical aspects.

Have Your Inventory Well in Advance

It doesn't matter what you're selling, you want to make sure you have the inventory you want to sell in your hands well in advance from the event date. You don't want to be doing things last minute here. If you're selling clothes and you place an order from your vendor that's set to arrive on Friday and your pop-up shop event is the next day on Saturday, that's a recipe for failure. What if there's a delay in shipping? What if one of your boxes gets lost or damaged during transit? What if you have to sign for the order and you're not available? You're also not going to have much time to sort through your items and get them organized. Be as proactive as possible and get things ordered as soon as you can to prevent scrambling, stress, and failure before the event even starts.

What Are the Logistics of the Event?

Whatever it is that you're selling, you need to think about the amount that you're going to order and where you're going to ship it to. For example, if you're ordering a lot of products for this event, then it would make more sense for you to ship the items directly to the event. However, the event might not open until the day before or even the day of for you to set everything up. They might not allow you to ship your products directly to the event. In that case, you might have to ship your products directly to your home. In this case, you're going to have to think about transportation. Are you going to be able to fit everything in your car? If not, you're going to need to rent a box truck or van so that you can fit everything, or you can hire a courier service. Essentially, this is a service that will transport a small shipment that can fit inside of a cargo van locally. So if you're in the same metropolitan area where the event will be held, this can be a good option for you. Like I mentioned earlier, you don't want to wait until the last minute to order everything just in case there are delays. Storage is another factor you're going to have to think about because of this. Will you be able to store all of your additional products at your home until the date of the event comes? If not, you do have a couple of options. You can rent a storage facility and store everything there. The other option is to ship everything to a cross-dock. Essentially, there are companies that can receive your shipment, store it, and then ship it out to another location when the time comes. So you could place your order and have it shipped to a cross-dock where it will stay until it is then sent to the place where the event is being held. You might already have everything you need supply-wise for the event, but if not, logistics are something that you need to think through.

Have All of Your Stock Organized

Another benefit to getting your stock in ahead of time is that you can be organized before the event occurs. You want to think about how you'll stock your pop-up shop. What items will you put out on display and how many? What items will you take off of display if you have less room than you initially planned for? You also have to think about your backstock. Will you leave everything on display and grab it from backstock when a customer wants to purchase a particular item? Or will you replenish items as they're bought? Either way, you need to think about this and have things organized properly. You don't want a bunch of random items in the same box. For example, if you're selling candles, you'd want each scent to be in its own box or storage compartment. This way when you need to grab more candles because people are buying them, you'll easily be able to find what you're looking for. You also want to have things spread out horizontally and not vertically when it comes to your backstock room. You might be limited with the amount of space that you have, but do your best to not stack different products on top of each other. So if you have a different scented candle in each box and you stack your boxes 5 high, what happens when you need the scent that's on the bottom of the stack? You now have to double-work yourself to get to the bottom of that stack. Sure, you might be limited on space and some items might have to be stacked on top of each other out of necessity. It's important to think about what sells the best and the worst so that you can keep the worst-selling items at the bottom of the stack. If you're selling clothing, then you have an additional layer of complexity to think about. You not only have the particular item, but you also have different sizes for each clothing item. So think about how you'll want to keep things organized. If you have the space for it, then you could get each unique item separate and have each size for that item be separated as well. If not, you'll at least want to separate each item as best you can.

What Do You Want the Flow of Your Shop to Be?

Your shop might be as simple as a fold-out table and if that's the case, then you're not going to have a ton of room left for creativity. However, if you have a bigger space, such as 10'x10' or 20'x20,' then you do have some room to work with, and thinking about your setup is important. You'll know how much space you're going to have ahead of time, so it's a good idea to draw out a rough sketch for how you want to set things up. When you're physically setting things up, you may notice that you don't like how things look in person compared to your original sketch. That's totally fine and you can change things, but coming up with a sketch will help to save you time when you are setting things up. So do you want your checkout stand to be in the back corner of your area or off to one side in the middle or front of your area? You can set things up where people will walk around your area with products surrounding them on both sides and then they are led to the checkout stand. You also want to have things set up in a way to where it's not going to impede other people who are shopping if the line does get backed up. You want to make sure that there's enough width for two people to walk down a lane if need be so that things aren't so cramped. It's up to you to design your pop-up shop how you want, but these are some ideas that you'll want to consider. How you set up your pop-up shop is very important. This is not a garage sale after all where people don't care about the aesthetics of the setup and are just looking for a good deal. In this case, you have other people that you're competing with and you need to compel people to want to take action and buy what it is that you're offering. You want to make your shop have a certain aura to it that makes people feel special, so that way they can feel that same type of way whenever they buy and use your products.

How Long Will You Have for Set Up?

Typically, you'll be able to set up your shop either the day before the event or the day of. This goes without saying, but if you're limited to the day of, you'll need to get there well in advance from when the place opens. Usually, the venue will make the sellers get there at a certain time to set up so that way there's less chaos when customers start to arrive. The thing about this is that it will give you a limited amount of time to set things up. You might want to rearrange things 2 or 3 times after seeing it in person to get everything just right. This is why you need to think ahead of time with how you want your initial setup to be so that you'll save time and can quickly tweak things as needed after you get everything set up. If you're able to come in the day before and set everything up, then you'll have more of a luxury with time, but it's still a good idea to plan ahead. What you don't want to do is just assume that you'll have plenty of time and worst case scenario you can just sling something together if you're crunched for time. Doing this can make your shop look sloppy and hinder your sales. A good approach is to give yourself more time than you initially think. So if you think you can get everything set up in 2 hours, it's not a bad idea to double that and give yourself 4 hours to get everything set up properly.

What Supplies Will You Need?

You've been thinking about your blueprint and how long it will take you to get everything set up. You've planned out and ordered any items you want to sell well in advance. The products that you're selling aren't the only physical items that you need to think about. You'll need to bring other supplies with you to be able to properly present your items to potential customers. I'm talking about things such as tables and clothing racks, as these are things that will not be provided to you by the venue in most cases. In addition to the basics, you need to think about things that will help to spruce up the basics. For instance, sure a basic fold-out table will get the job done as you can present your products on the table and leave it at that.

Doing this, however, would be a missed opportunity. There are some things that you can do to make your area look much more eye-appealing for anyone who walks by. You could put a table cloth over the table and the cloth could be a color that goes along with the colors of your brand. Now instead of having an ugly plain table, your setup will instantly look nice. Let's say you're selling clothes, candles, or something else along those lines. You can use tiered stands to create different levels on your table. So instead of all of your products sitting flat on your table, some of your products will sit higher than others. This will not only make your products look more aesthetically pleasing, but it will make it easier to take in everything that you have to offer. Instead of seeing a table with a bunch of candles on it that are all on the same level, people will more easily be able to see the different scents that you have to offer because your products are layered. It's not like it's going to take a bunch of extra time or money to be able to set something like this up, but it will go a long way in separating yourself from everyone else, and it will make a difference in the amount of sales that you make. Another good idea is to get clothing racks if you sell clothes. This will make things better for yourself and the customers. You'll be able to put more items out in your shop, and it will make things easier for your customers to be able to look through when they're deciding what they want to buy. The next thing you want to think about is a pop-up tent. This will be dependent on the venue itself. Some venues will be inside and this won't be necessary in those instances. Some events will be outside, but they'll have covered spots so you'll be good to go in those cases as well. However, you may find yourself at an outdoor event or outside of someone's business where you won't have any coverage at all. Depending on what the weather is, you may be good as you are. If it's really hot, cold, windy, raining, or even super sunny, it's a good idea to bring your own pop-up tent that you can set up to help protect your products and customers from the elements. People will want to stop by and see what you have to offer simply as a way to get out of the cold or whatever else the weather has brought in that day. The good news about a pop-up tent is that they're easy to set up and take down so it's not a big hassle. A pop-up tent could easily cost you anywhere between $150 to $350 or more depending on the size. You can also buy tent walls to have coverage on the sides, which is something that I highly recommend that you do. If you're dealing with elements such as the cold or wind, then the walls will help to block this and make it more enjoyable for people to stick around. If not, people won't stay as long and will tend to flock to areas where they can stay warm. Another cool thing you can do with tents is brand them. You can have the top of the tent and the walls branded with your company name, logo, and colors. Customizing a tent will be an additional expense and it's not a necessity, but it's another step that you can take to stand apart from everyone else. Lastly, consider bringing shopping bags for your customers. Shopping bags will usually not be provided by the venue, so it's a good idea to take care of this for your customers. You can buy generic bags or you can take things one step further and buy customized bags to rep your brand. Now when people are moving around after purchasing from you, they are now a walking advertisement.

What Types of Payment Will You Accept?

There isn't a bigger way to miss out on a sale than you not accepting a certain form of payment. Imagine a customer wanting to make a purchase who walks up to you with cash, and you say, "Sorry I don't accept cash." The customer walks away and spends their money elsewhere and you just missed out on a sale. This is the last thing that you want to happen. You've done all of the hard work up to this point to make that sale, so it's critical to accept as many different forms of payment as you possibly can. So in regards to cash, it's important to bring change with you. Be sure that you could break a $100 or $50 bill. Bring coins with you as well so that you can give exact change. These are the things you need to think about when you're going to accept multiple forms of payment. Don't just assume that your customers will have the exact bill that they need. You want to make things easy for the customer to spend their money. Cash isn't the only form of payment that you want to accept. The most common form of payment that people use nowadays is credit cards. You'll need a way to accept credit card payments if you currently don't have a way to do so. If you use Shopify to help run your online store, you can order a POS (point of sale) system from Shopify. There are other options available to you in case you don't use that system. You can do an online search for a POS system and see if any particular brand piques your interest. Square has a good POS system as well that's worth looking into. Typically the way these companies work is the actual system itself will either be free or very inexpensive. Then they'll take a small percentage of each sale that you make such as 2.5%. Having to pay fees isn't something I'm sure you're excited about, but you're not going to be able to get around this when you're taking payments from a credit card. Accepting cash and credit cards still isn't enough though. It's a good idea to accept other forms of payment such as Cash App, Venmo, Apple Pay, Zelle, and PayPal. This way you'll have every basis covered and you won't have to worry about missing out on a sale.

Chapter 5: How to Get People to Come to Your Pop-Up Shop

The cool thing about a pop-up shop is that the event itself can draw out a lot of people so you might not have to worry about people stopping by. Why leave things up to chance though when you could take matters into your own hands and ensure that you have a steady stream of people stopping by to see what you have to offer? In this chapter, you're not only going to learn how you can draw a crowd but also make the most of the people who decide to purchase from you.

Create a Solid Offer Just for the Event

The first thing that you want to do is create a good deal that will give people a reason to come and check out what you have to offer. Sure some people who you know will want to come out to support you, but that's not how most people are going to operate. They care about what's in it for themselves. So if they care about what you're selling and you give them an offer they can't refuse, they're going to come out. That's why it's important to offer a special deal just for the event. People aren't going to go out of their way to come to something unless they have a good reason to, so this is the perfect way to do just that. Your offer can be anything that you want, such as buy one get one half off. Or buy 3 of these particular products and get a 4th one free. Another example is get 10% off of your order when you use the promo code "Pop-Up" at the checkout. Again, remember to think about items that you have a backstock of that you want to get rid of. The offering can be as big or small as you'd like for it to be, but it needs to be something. And you also want to give this same offering to your online audience so that way no one feels left out. Some of your followers are in a different area from where you live so it won't be possible for them to come. However, they'll still feel special if they're able to take advantage of the deal.

Pass Out Flyers on the Weekends

Making flyers is going to be an additional expense, so don't feel as if you have to do this. There are free ways that you can go about promoting your pop-up shop, but this is a good way to go about things. Essentially what you want to do is create flyers centered around your brand, the products that you sell, and the offer that you're going to use for the event. Then you want to go out on a Saturday in a general vicinity to where the event that you're selling will be and start passing out your flyers. This is the most effective way to go about this because people who are already out will be more likely to come out on the day of the event. I recommend doing this every Saturday for 3 or 4 weeks prior to when your event will be so that you can hit up as many people as possible.

Promote Yourself on Social Media

This is a similar concept to that of passing out physical flyers. The difference is this time that you're essentially making a digital flyer and posting it for your followers to see. The mistake you don't want to make here is to only post about your pop-up shop once leading up to the event. You want to post about the event multiple times starting one month out if possible. Post about the event once per week until you're a week away from the event. Then you're going to post 3 times during that week. Your posts don't need to be anything special, just more so to serve as a reminder of what's about to come. You'll want to promote your special event offer and be sure to post about this not just on your business profiles, but your personal profiles as well to help expand your reach. Once you're at the event you don't want to shrug your shoulders and assume you've done all that you could. There's still more you can do to help promote your pop-up shop during the day of the event. You can post on your story throughout the day of you setting up and just being at your shop. The other thing you can do is go live as well, as this will send an alert to all of your followers and it's a great way to gain exposure.

Use a Promo Sign Outside of Your Shop

People who are already at the event and haven't seen any of your promotional materials won't know about the special that you're offering. You need a way to make your offer known to people who are walking by to help draw them in. The best way to do this is by having a promotional sign that says what your offer is. You want to use something that's on the bigger side that will stand out, such as an a-frame sign. Using something that's the size of a piece of paper won't do you any good, and as long as your offer is compelling enough, it will get people to check out what you have to offer.

Make the Most of Customers that Stop By

I'm sure you know that it's harder to acquire a customer than to keep an existing customer. The goal of the shop is to make money, but also have a wave of new customers that will continue to buy from you in the future. The way that you can do this is by collecting email addresses from people who stop by. If you already have an email list, this is a great way to continue to build your list and stay in contact with new people from your shop. It doesn't matter if people buy or not. If they're showing interest at the very least, give them a business card or ask for their email so they can receive future promotions. You don't want people to just walk as this will add up to a lot of missed revenue as the years go on.

Don't Sit There Bored on Your Phone

The last piece of advice I have for you when you're trying to draw people in is to not sit there looking bored on your phone. This gives off the vibe that your shop is dead and makes it look like you don't want to be there. Instead, stand at the edge of your area and give people a friendly hello as they walk by. When people are in your shop looking around, it's okay to ask them if they need help finding anything. What's not okay is to hover around people and not give them the space that they need. I know that I hate it when I'm the only person in a store and the worker won't leave me alone! Don't make that same mistake in your shop.

Conclusion

Pop-up shops are a great way to stack some extra cash and new customers into your business. Don't be fooled however into thinking that just because you have a pop-up shop that you're automatically going to be swimming in the cash because of it. Having a successful pop-up shop requires a lot of planning, work, and diligence. If you go about it correctly though, then it will absolutely be worth the effort. The only variable it comes down to is you. I'm sure though that because you took initiative and read this book, you'll be willing to put that same level of desire into your shop. If you do that, then you're sure to see success. Best of luck!